Danielle King

Dear Danielle
God is ever so faithful and watches over His word to perform it. Keep on trusting Him, Jeremiah 1:12 — Be blessed always
Emefa

Beyond
the
Shame!

Beyond
the
Shame!

Arise, shine; 'for thy light is come, and the glory of the Lord is risen upon thee. For behold darkness shall cover the earth, and gross darkness the people: but the Lord shall arise upon thee, and his glory shall be seen upon thee (Isaiah 60:1-2)

Emefa Toppar
Foreword by Bishop Richard Aryee

www.Lulu.com

Beyond The Shame
Copyright ©2010 Emefa Toppar
www.emefatoppar.com
etoppar@gmail.com

Unless otherwise stated, all scripture quotations are taken from the King James Version (KJV) of the Bible.

ISBN: 978-1-4457-8939-2

All rights reserved under international copyright law. Written Permission must be secured from the Publisher to use or reproduce any part of this book, except for brief quotations in critical reviews or articles.

Printed in the United States of America

www.lulu.com

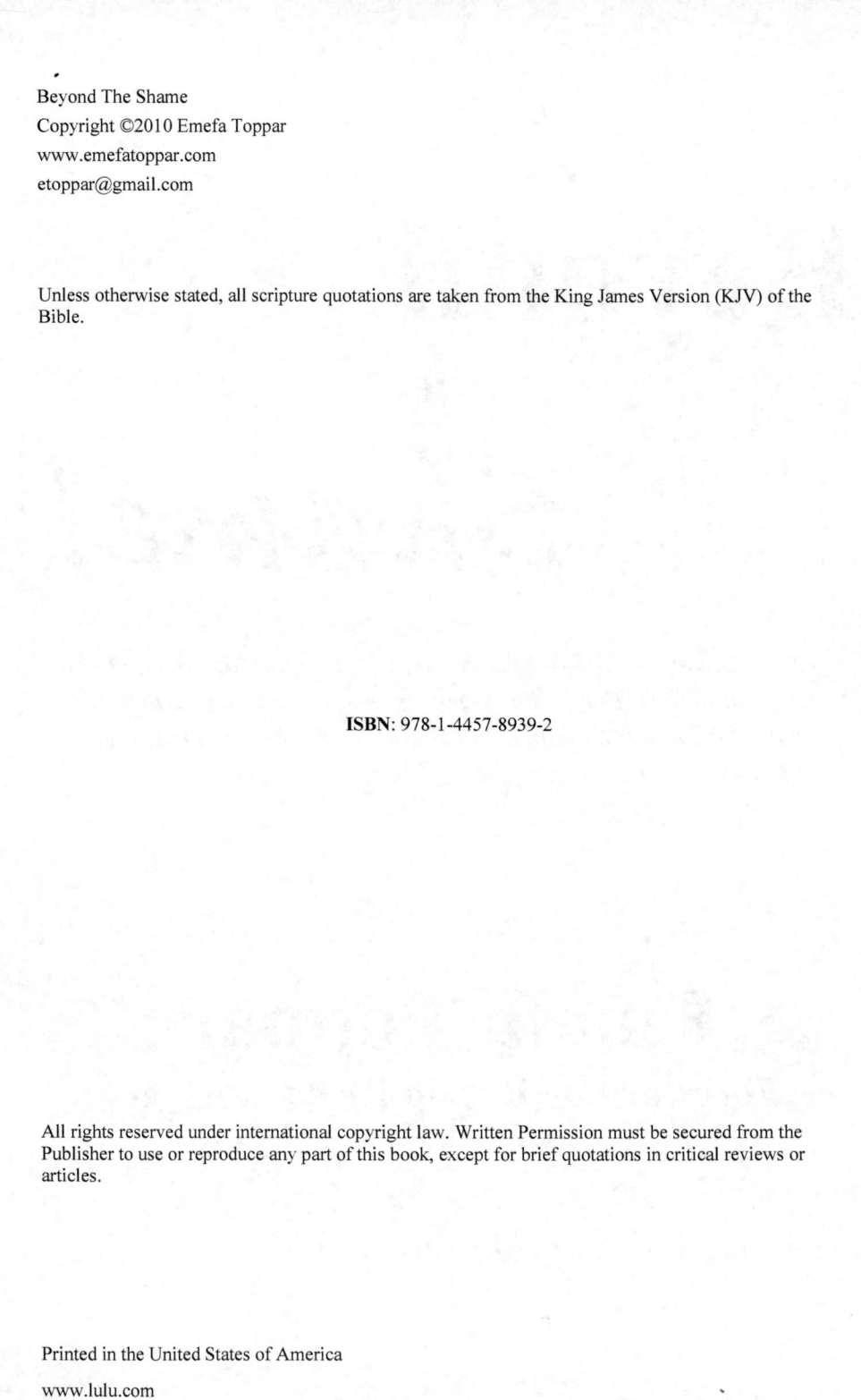

DEDICATION

With lots of love and appreciation to my parents,
Hendrie and Grace Toppar.
God could not have blessed me with a better
Dad and Mum!
Thank you for all the years you dried my tears,
calmed my anxieties and just loved me better!
I pray God's grace over you
May the Lord exalt you
May the Lord honour you
Love, Yacoba,
Your precious daughter - the first one!

Isaiah 50:7

*For the Lord GOD will help me; therefore shall I not be confounded: therefore have I set my face like a flint, and **I know that I shall not be ashamed**.*

Matthew 9:22

*But Jesus turned him about and when he saw her, he said, **"Daughter, be of good comfort; thy faith hath made thee whole"** and the woman was made whole from that hour.*

Daughter, There Is No Shame

So lift up your head, woman of Zion,
Daughter of Jerusalem, My daughter!
I see in the distance the outstretched arms of the Lord,
Wide open to draw you into the embrace of His love and power,

To tell you how precious and beautiful you are to Him,
To give you beauty for ashes. For He has preserved you for such a time as this,
That you may go out and boldly declare in confidence and trust, the unwavering love of the lord.

The time has come to lay aside every weight
of guilt, shame and pain.
It is the season of joy; its' the season you have been waiting for; it is the season to spread out your wings and fly up –

Soar up with healing in your wings!
Because of the love you have received at My feet, you will be able to share My love with so many who are sometimes bound by their fears and at a loss as to why I am silent concerning their troubles.

You can whisper words of love and encouragement to them.
You can remind them of My eternal love for them, whisper strength to their weary bones, and they will rise in hope and power to be all that I have called them to be.

There is no shame with her, whose hand remains in the palm of her Lord, trusting, believing, praying, hoping, for her expectation shall not be cut off. Now is time for your redemption, you who have been left behind.

For I determine the times and the seasons, that the purposes for which I have chosen and called you will be fulfilled.

Run, my daughter, run into My outstretched arms; for I have called you for a specific reason, and you will fulfil your destiny.

As you have been strengthened, so shall you strengthen your brethren who are in bondage!

Emefa Toppar
October 2009

Dedicated with God's love to You!

1 Corinthians 9:27

But I keep under my body, and bring it into subjection: lest that by any means, when I have preached to others, I myself should be a castaway

Contents

Foreword xv
Acknowledgements xvii
Introduction xix
1. As We Assemble Again in Christ 1
2. God's Faithfulness Over the Years 11
3. Waiting Eagerly for the Phone Call 17
4. A Friendship Begins to Develop 25
5. A Marriage Proposal 31
6. Striving for Godly Peace 39
7. The Difficult Decision 45
8. Broken in Spirit, Yet Daring to Trust Again 49
9. The Healing Rain of God's Love 57
10. Nuggets of Godly Wisdom 63

Foreword

It is a joy to be invited to write the foreword to Emefa Toppar's book, *Beyond the Shame*. Emefa Toppar is a dedicated Christian and a pastor with Lighthouse Chapel International. Like many other Christians, she has had times when she felt the Lord had abandoned her in her times of distress but, I believe this book is a story shared to encourage you not to think in the wrong way when things are not going right, but allow yourself to be transformed into a new person by the renewing of your mind.

This book will touch you as it reveals her heart and her desire to see you rise up from dejection, despair, pain and anguish into the person God has intended you to be. Her desire is for you to know that insecurities and pain can prevent you from pressing on into the blessing God has in store for you.

Beyond the Shame, has been burning in Emefa for years and I pray it will serve as encouragement to someone who will determine to let go of the past, and find strength to move on as the future is full of hope. God is extending His grace to you, do accept it.

July 22, 2010

Bishop Richard Aryee
Senior Pastor
Lighthouse Chapel International
London, United Kingdom

Acknowledgements

My Lord Jesus, who chose to love me. How great is the Lord my God!

With love to my dear siblings, Jiffa, Lorlor and Kafui. I hold closely to my heart and treasure our childhood memories. The rod was not spared, but laced with generous helpings of love, we were able to laugh on! How good God has been to us; We can climb every mountain. Love, *Emefa*.

With love to Kow and Jay, my precious brother- and sister-in-law, respectively. To my nieces and nephews, Theone, Anpra, Megan, Jermaine, Ivan and Jerrell – my heart curls up with love at the thought of you. Hugs and love, *Mummy Emefa*.

To Esther Baah Amoako, for so many years of prayer, love and faithfulness – for when we laughed and also when we cried, and for sharing your lovely daughters Zoe and Jasmin with me. Thus far has the Lord brought us. I love you.

My heartfelt gratitude to my pastor, my father, my friend, Bishop Richard Aryee, and to his wife Lady Pastor Linda Aryee. At last I can laugh again; my soul rejoices because I can testify that it has been worth holding on to God. Thank you for loving me through this time and for not giving up on me. God bless your family. I love you too, *Emef.*

With much appreciation and love to my bishop, my father, Bishop Dag Heward-Mills. You continue to bless, teach and inspire me so greatly! Nine years after telling you about writing a book (Sheffield Camp, UK, 2001), and after reading your book, *'The Art of Hearing: Following the Voice of God'*, I have finally obeyed God! I thank God for your life!

To Lady Reverend Adelaide Heward-Mills, thank you for your heart's desire to make a way for women to rise up, out of our own limitations. You are compassionate, charming and gracious. I'd like so much to be like you!

Acknowledgements

With special thanks and love to my church family, the Lighthouse Chapel International! Especially to Reverend Jude Baiden. God has been so faithful through the years. Love you!

To wonderful memories and beautiful lifetime friendships developed at Aburi Girls' Secondary School. Esther, Adina, Louisa, Woseila, Maame Serwaa, Rita-Audrey, Alfreda, Shola, Leticia and others – your love and support is amazing. That hill was worth climbing! Hugs and love!

My dear friends Eliz and Kurankyi Dadson, and Yacoba Godwyll – you were there when it mattered most. May God richly bless you!

I am so grateful to you all and others not mentioned here. It is a blessed life!

Introduction

Has the Lord as much delight in burnt offerings and sacrifices, as in obeying the voice of the Lord? Behold, to obey is better than sacrifice, And to heed than the fat of rams.

1 Samuel 15:22

It has taken me a long time to obey God by writing what I believe He asked me to.

I have finally run out of excuses not to write and, painfully aware that the Lord had been silent for a while, I am humbled that God has given me enough grace to do what He asked me to do several years ago, confirmed in several ways.

I am tired of living a life below God's best for me, of not bearing fruit as I should, to glorify the Lord (Jhn 15:8: "Herein is my Father glorified that ye bear much fruit: so shall ye be my disciples"), of having the potential but yet not achieving what am capable of. Could this be a result of my disobedience to God's urging me to write books that will help somebody else, books that will bring healing to others?

This book is based on the true story of how, several years ago, I made the decision not to go ahead with a planned marriage. I had prayed and sought the face of the Lord for His peace concerning my decision for a year. At the end of the year, I felt able to leave a relationship with a good man because I believed, then and now, that my journey with him was not one of marriage but was rather one of good friendship, united by the love of Christ which we had both received – *agape* love and *phileo* love.[1]

---

[1] Love (*agape*) from Strong's concordance:
There are several Greek words for "love" that are regularly referred to in Christian circles.
- *Agape*: In the New Testament, *agapē* is charitable, selfless, altruistic, and unconditional. It is parental love, seen as creating goodness in the world; it is the way God is seen to love humanity, and it is seen as the kind of love that Christians aspire to have for one another.

Introduction

It was a difficult decision and one that I did not take lightly, but it was a decision that had to be made.[2]

This decision led me through several thorny and difficult paths. There were times when I felt so alone and so misunderstood, craving love and acceptance.

There were times when I felt that the Lord had abandoned me in a pit of sorrow, to a life of sadness, and that it was indeed over for me, especially in terms of marriage.

This story tells of my journey through pain and guilt, as well as moments of despair, to a place of eternal peace and joy in the Lord, a place where I am confident in the love and grace of God, which is all I need to be all that God desires me to be.

The Reason for What I Went Through

The experiences I have been privileged to go through are not just about me but are for the edification of others as well. It is no longer my story alone but a story that, when shared, could liberate others from wrong thinking and enable them to be transformed by the renewing of their minds (Rom 12:2: "And be not conformed to this world: but be transformed by the renewing of your mind, that ye may prove what is that good, and acceptable and perfect, will of God").

My story could help you to stop thinking

- *It is your fault that you are still unmarried!*
- *There must be something wrong with you because you did not marry when most of your friends were marrying.*
- *You must be a very bad person, to have rejected a very good person.*
- *It is over for you because you did not marry a particular person.*

- *Phileo*: Also used in the New Testament, *phileo* is a human response to something that is found to be delightful. Also known as "brotherly love."

[2]Dag Heward-Mills, *The Art of Leadership* (Accra, Ghana/London, UK: Parchment House, 2003) 239–243.

I also share this story so that others may rise up and be all that God has called them to be – learning from the past, letting go of the past, and excelling in their God-given assignments.

How can that happen if somebody in the chain of God's blessings refuses to pass along the baton of blessing, due to that person's own insecurities and inability to see beyond the present circumstances?

This book is not an attempt to justify any action but rather to shine the torch of God's love, light up a flame of hope in your life and enable you to be all that God has called you to be.

My story may be less painful than yours; my story may not equal yours, even in the guilt and shame I have carried around all these years. But I pray that as I have been open and honest and shared my pain, my guilt, my sense of utter hopelessness, you will be comforted and know, or be reminded, that God is a God of second chances, that God loves you with an everlasting love (Jer 31:3: "Yea, I have loved thee with an everlasting love").

You will know that there is hope for you, for you will rise up again like a tree which, when cut down, sprouts again at the scent of water (Job 14: 7–9: "For there is hope for a tree, if it be cut down, that it will sprout again, and that the tender branch thereof will not cease. Though the root therefore wax old in the earth, and the stock thereof die in the ground; Yet through the scent of water it will bud, and bring forth boughs like a plant").

As a woman, one of the major decisions you will make concerns the issue of marriage. Sometimes a decision may cause you to have certain experiences – some pleasant and others not so pleasant. Some of these decisions may take you through the wilderness of life for a while.

But whatever it is, our God is in Heaven, and He would like me to reassure you that He is not holding you for ransom for not marrying one particular person. He would like you to move on in life, in your walk with Him.

God says that, should there be a need for forgiveness, He definitely has forgiven you. It is not up to anybody else to determine that – but for you to receive His forgiveness and move on to another level in your life.

There are greater heights ahead, higher mountains to climb and still more land to be taken for the Lord. There are more souls to be

Introduction

won for the kingdom of God. There are more messages to be preached and more churches to be established (Dan 12:3: "And they that be wise shall shine as the brightness of the firmament; and they that turn many to righteousness as the stars for ever and ever").

However, you need to be confident in God's love and trust that so long as you do not take any step without consulting Him, so long as you include Him in any decisions you make, then the course of your life has been directed by Him.

- *Sometimes through rugged terrain*
- *Sometimes through the wilderness*
- *Sometimes through green pastures*

You need to have faith in the direction of your path (Psa 37:23: "The steps of a good man are ordered by the Lord: and he delighteth in his way").

This is for you, the woman who desires but has not yet experienced the blessing of marriage for whatever reason. This is for you, the woman who has felt left out as the years have passed by. For you, the Christian woman who loves the Lord so passionately, yet also desires to marry.

It is okay to have such a need; it is a good desire to have. It is a spiritual desire – don't be ashamed of your need (1Cor 7:2: "Nevertheless to avoid fornication, let every man have his own wife, and let every woman have her own husband").

Honestly, you are allowed to have such desires; they do not make you any less spiritual. Just do not allow these desires to overshadow your every waking moment! Find something to do for the Lord and serve Him with zeal and passion.

So, this is especially for you, who perhaps may be plagued by thoughts of decisions made years ago, and the effects of those decisions now.

How long are you going to continue moaning for what is not and what might have been? You sought the peace of God and acted on it; that is what matters.

Even if you didn't seek God diligently, and made a mistake in your decision, God still forgives, and His compassions fail not; they are new every morning (Lam 3:22–23: "It is of the Lord's mercies that we are not consumed, because his compassions fail not. They are new every morning: great is thy faithfulness").

There is a higher purpose in all this than the fact that you feel lonely, bereft of a particular blessing. The Lord allowed this set of circumstances, to enable His higher purpose to be achieved.

The Lord allowed what happened, in the way it happened, for a reason. There is a reason for what you went through (Isa 55:8: "For my thoughts are not your thoughts, neither are your ways my ways, saith the Lord, For as the heavens are higher than the earth, so are my ways higher than your ways, and my thoughts than your thoughts").

So great is the measure of our Father's love towards you.

My Prayer for You

I pray that the Lord will cause His unwavering love to be a banner and shield over you as you read.

I pray that the healing rain of God's love and care for you will wash away any deception the enemy of our soul has entangled you in.

May you know God's liberating love.

May you rise up in God's kingdom to do great things for him, not hampered in any way by any negative thoughts about your ability or qualification to do so.

I pray that any kind of shackle of deception that has held you back, and caused you to look down in shame, be broken by the precious blood of the Lord Jesus (Ps 25:3: "Yea, let none that wait on thee be ashamed").

It's my prayer for you, should you desire to marry a believer, that as you have borne your cross of being unmarried, that God – who is not a respecter of persons but who rewards those who diligently seek Him – might reward you for all the years that the locust has stolen (Joel 2:25: "And I will restore to you the years that the locust hath eaten, the cankerworm, and the caterpillar, and the palmerworm, my great army which I sent among you").

May the Lord honour you.

May the Lord reward you in a beautiful way, cause you to lift up your head, smile, and walk in confidence as you come boldly before His throne of Grace to find help in time of need (Hbr 4:16: "Let us therefore come boldly unto the throne of grace, that we may obtain mercy, and find grace to help in time of need").

Introduction

Pearls of Life

It is better to trust in the Lord than to put confidence in man.

Psalm 118:8

Trust in the Lord with all thine heart; and lean not on unto thine own understanding. In all thy ways acknowledge him, and he shall direct thy paths.

Proverbs 3:5–6

Behold, God is my salvation; I will trust, and not be afraid: for the LORD JEHOVAH is my strength and my song; he also is become my salvation

Isaiah 12:2

Trust ye in the Lord forever: for in the Lord JEHOVAH is everlasting strength:

Isaiah 26:4

1

AS WE ASSEMBLE AGAIN IN CHRIST

Not forsaking the assembling of ourselves together as the manner of some is; but exhorting one another: and so much the more, as you see the day approaching.

Hebrews 10:25

It was the summer of 1999, and the members of my church were looking forward to lots of Christian activities and fun. One particular planned activity that summer was a three-day retreat in Devon, in the United Kingdom, with our presiding bishop. It was the first time that such a programme had been organized in the United Kingdom for my church, and we were all excited.

There was a lot of joy and expectation as we prepared for this time of spiritual renewal with God. It was also an opportunity to meet with other believers, away from the stress of everyday life. It promised to be a summer of God's peace and joy. I had never been to such a programme, and I was amazed at how far God had brought me in terms of what I was willing to sacrifice in order to draw closer to Him.

Secretly, the unmarried ones amongst us, (at least the ones I had spoken with) hoped to meet some Christian brethren – for who knows what the Lord will do when we are all gathered?

Dear Lord, I also prayed in the quietness of my room, *as I draw closer to You, may I also meet a godly man, someone who loves You and is determined to seek You first in all things. Someone who desires to work for You and who will accept and love me as I am, whilst praying for me to be all that You have called me to be.*

I had begun a love relationship with God again, since coming to London in 1995, and my joy in the things of God seemed to be increasing. I had fallen in love with Jesus all over again.

I sometimes wondered how that could have been; that was not part of my plan when I had left the shores of Ghana for greener pastures.

My planned agenda did not include spiritual progress in the ways of God at all. It was actually supposed to be an escape to freedom – freedom to go out with whomever I liked, freedom to do what I wanted, freedom to pursue my ambitious desire to climb the corporate ladder very quickly, and freedom not to go to church every Sunday. I had dreamt of weekends away with a boyfriend in Switzerland, Holland or France, because I felt that my life had not been interesting enough in the past.

Like a lot of people, I had tried to be a good Christian without actually understanding all about Jesus dwelling in me, or about the need to grow in the ways of God. If anything, I felt that the Lord owed me for having tried to obey Him.

My Christian life until then had all been about obeying rules and trying so hard to be holy, without actually enjoying the walk with Jesus. Of course, I hadn't known then what I was missing!

But God in His mercies stopped me, and before any of that could happen, I found myself in a Bible-believing, prayerful, tongue-speaking, active and alive church (Jer 29:11: "For I know the thoughts that I think toward you, saith the Lord, thoughts of peace, and not of evil, to give you an expected end").

I am so grateful to God that my foolish dreams did not have a chance to materialize. For the truth is, God loves us with an everlasting love and is always looking for an opportunity to be a blessing to us (Rom 8:38–39: "For I am persuaded, that neither death, nor life, nor angels, nor principalities, nor powers, nor things present, nor things to come, Nor height, nor depth, nor any other creature, shall be able to separate us from the love of God which is in Christ Jesus our Lord").

So there I was, for the first time, going away on a spiritual retreat.

Devon: A Spiritual Journey

I woke up early the next day, Friday morning. I spent the first part of the day in prayer, worship and reading my Bible – my quiet time with the Lord. I checked my luggage again to ensure that I had everything I needed. It was a very beautiful day, with clear, sunny skies.

My friends Yvette and Bernard picked me up from home, and we met up with the others in front of church. There was an air of excitement all around.

"Emefa!" someone called me from behind.

I turned around, and there was my friend Sam, all the way from the United States of America.

"Hello! What a blessing to see you here," I said to him joyfully as I gave him a big hug. I had known Sam for about five years. He had been a colleague of my childhood friend Ruth at University. They had both trained as accountants afterwards.

"Ruth should see you now," Sam remarked. "She spent time praying that you would know the joys of the Lord in a more fulfilling way."

"Indeed, she will be chuffed," I laughed.

After chatting a bit about life abroad and the joy of meeting up again, we promised to catch up on each other's news, and Sam went to talk to some other people that he knew.

The camp overseer finally managed to get us all on board amidst a lot of laughter and joy. One of the pastors said a short prayer, and by ten o'clock, we were off to Devon.

Yvette sat next to me, and we reminisced about God's goodness and faithfulness all these years.

"Emefa," Yvette said, with a hint of regret in her voice, "if I had known that being deeply involved in the things of God was so fulfilling and exciting, I would have been more serious about God years ago."

I agreed with her totally; instead of being boring, church was proving to be an exciting and fun place. I shared with her again that whilst in University I had not been a serious Christian. My time at University had seemed an opportunity to find out about the fun others seemed to be having in the world – and apart from that, one could not really appreciate the joy and genuineness of the believers. Their lifestyle appeared boring and unattractive – surely, there were other more interesting things to do than the prayer meetings they seemed to have all the time?

I wondered why we had not discovered the exciting and liberating truth of walking with the Lord earlier. I was reminded then of the story in the scriptures about the woman at the well (Jhn 4:7–30). She was seeking for things that could not satisfy, but as soon as she perceived who Jesus was, she went and told everyone about Him, and many believed in Him because of the word of the woman who testified.

Somebody lifted up a praise song then; I think it must have been "All Things Are Possible," by Darlene Zschech.[1] Since my decision to get serious again about my relationship with God, I had been imagining myself as a worship leader one day, and I joined in wholeheartedly.

(It would take me some time and some humbling moments to realize God has not called me to leading worship at this time. Thanks be to God who reveals the truth about ourselves to us – Jhn 8:32: "and you will know the truth and the truth will set you free.")

After travelling for about two hours, we stopped at one of the motorway services for a break. It was good to get off the coach and stretch our legs. I went across to speak with Pastor John, who was in charge of the church worker group that I belonged to. "I can see you are really looking forward to the retreat," he teased me when he saw me. "You are going to return a much-anointed vessel, ready to do more for the Lord."

"Oh, Pastor John!" I exclaimed. "I am just so blessed to be part of this. This Christian walk is becoming more and more fulfilling."

We chatted for a little while longer, and he encouraged me to be alert and receive with an open and willing heart all that our bishop would be teaching during the camp.

All too soon, the break was over, and we were back on board heading for Devon.

I started reading my Bible but fell asleep after a few pages, I guess nature was taking its toll; the past few days had been exciting and tiring.

I woke up to the sound of singing; somebody was obviously still going strong.

Looking out of the window, I noticed the change in the landscape to rolling green hills. We had definitely left the city behind, and the countryside was so beautiful; there were lots of trees and greenery, and the fields were lovely, with sheep grazing here and there. I even noticed a few scattered horses. The Devon countryside reminded me of

---

[1] "All Things Are Possible," © 1997 Darlene Zschech/Hillsongs Publishing.

Aburi in Ghana, where I had gone to high school; it too was very scenic and pleasant to the eyes.

Oh Lord, I prayed quietly in my heart, *may I experience all that You have to give me during this retreat.*

And also, a small, quiet voice could not resist whispering, *I do need to meet a godly man soon. Marriage is honourable, and I really would like to do it Your way, God. Who knows? It may happen at this camp.*

We quickly settled in when we arrived at the retreat centre where we were to spend the next few days. The first part of the camp was scheduled to begin that very evening, and we all hurried off to get ready.

The Lord Is Magnified

The next couple of days were so awesome; the presence of God in the worship services and the teaching meetings was just so strong. I was reminded of how glory filled the house of the Lord that King Solomon had built in Jerusalem, (2Chron 5:13: "and when they praised the Lord saying, 'He indeed is good for His loving kindness is everlasting,' then the house, of the Lord was filled with a cloud").

The teaching that weekend emphasized getting involved in missionary work, being the ones who would also lay aside our own desires and ambitions, to carry the good news of salvation to others.

Our bishop taught on being a missionary church; he encouraged us to consider becoming missionaries who would take the word of God to all the parts of the world in order that we would also fulfil the Great Commission (Mat 28:19–20: "Go ye therefore and make disciples of all nations, baptizing them in the name of the father and of the son and the Holy Spirit. Teaching them to observe all that I have commanded you; and lo, I am with you always, even to the end of the world").

The whole experience was a new and exhilarating one for me, and I could feel that I had indeed found a good thing in being introduced to this other aspect of Christianity – one of also contributing to taking the Gospel far and wide.

Oh Lord, I prayed, *may I not depart from what I have found! May I hold on to this joy that I have found in You. May the coming years be an opportunity for me to testify that indeed You are faithful.*

A Glimmer of Hope

All too soon it was over, and we were on the coach heading back to our various destinations with promises to keep in touch with one another.

It had been so hectic at the camp that my friend Sam and I had not had the opportunity to do more than exchange pleasantries as we hurried from one session to another, but he managed to sit by me on the way back to London. We each shared what had taken place for us at the camp and how blessed we had been to be part of it.

A few minutes into the journey, however, Sam turned to look at me quite seriously and said he needed to discuss something with me and that there was no better time than the present. I wondered what it could be.

"Are you in a relationship with anyone?" he asked me.

"Well," I answered, trying to come across as a very spiritual Christian sister who didn't spend every waking moment waiting and hoping for a husband, "good things come to those who wait.", (Psa 37:9: "but those that wait upon the Lord, they shall inherit the earth.")

"Of course good things come to those who wait upon the Lord," my friend answered. (Psa 84:11: "for the Lord God is a sun and shield: the Lord will give grace and glory: no good thing will He withhold from them that walk uprightly.") "But what does that mean, Emefa, in your current situation? You are either in a relationship – hopefully, unto marriage – or not."

"I am not in a relationship," I managed to answer, "but I am prayerfully expecting this will happen sooner rather than later."

He appeared to be lost in thought for a few seconds and then, as if carefully considering his words, said to me, "I would like to introduce you to a good friend of mine, someone I can really recommend to you. He is familiar with the charismatic style of worship and worships in a church similar to ours – a Bible-believing, prayerful, tongue-speaking, active and alive church. I know that's something you'd like. He is a good man and I think you'd like him."

I looked at Sam, thinking that would be great. But then alarm bells also began to ring in my ears. *What if he doesn't like me?* I wondered. *What if he doesn't think am spiritual enough? What if he doesn't think I would be a good wife for a serious Christian, someone desiring to do well in Christian leadership?*

My list of fears grew and grew. *What if his senior pastors do not approve of me and rather expect him to choose a wife from within their own congregation? What if people tell him that I had a failed relationship in University?*

What if people conclude that I couldn't find a man on my own and one had to be given to me?

And then, unlikely as it seemed then, I thought, *What if I don't like* him *in that kind of way?* The boy/girl way that paves the way to a lifetime commitment – because although my greatest joy would be to marry a committed Christian involved in the ministry, I also knew that there had to be something more in addition to this. The ultimate decision would be a result of God's peace on both sides – for this relationship would involve two spiritual people, (Col 3:15: "And let the peace of God rule in your hearts, to the which also ye are called in one body; and be ye thankful").

Initially I thought I would answer in the negative – that is, say no to my friend's request – the reason being that it takes so much out of you emotionally. You wonder if the person will like you and you'll like him when you meet. If it works out, everyone will be happy, but if it doesn't work out, there will be some feelings of pain and disappointment.

Later on, many years after, when some people made rather hurtful and insensitive comments about why I was still not married (especially the married ones), I would always wonder. *What have you suffered, what have you endured, what have you overcome in search of marriage?*

But then grace is always available from God to hold on to the truth of God's word and to move on regardless of my pain and shame (2Cor 4:8–9: "We are troubled on every side, yet not distressed; we are perplexed, but not in despair; Persecuted, but not forsaken, cast down, but not destroyed").

However, I was willing to try meeting Sam's friend. I believe I was gradually being transformed by the word of God and had come a bit further in the things of God than to let public opinion cloud my decision. Gone were the Mills and Boon daydreams of being approached by a *tall, dark, handsome man,* of looking across a packed room and suddenly *locking eyes with one particular gentleman.* Furthermore, surely a tried, tested and known brother in the Lord was better husband material than an exciting but unknown character of uncertain intentions.

So before we got back to London, I had agreed to let Sam introduce me to his friend David, a committed Christian involved in the ministry of the Lord Jesus. I was quietly smiling in my heart; I did not want to appear overeager, but, honestly, my heart was beating so fast and so loud that it was a wonder my friend didn't ask me if I was alright!

I was looking forward to telling the good news to my friend Yvette. I knew I would pick up the phone as soon as I got home to also chat to my dearest friend, Ruth. We would giggle like schoolgirls again. Something good and exciting was about to happen!

Sam initially wanted me to call his friend David in Accra, Ghana, but that was one thing I thought should be up to the gentleman! In Ghana we had always been taught that it was up to the man to make his intentions known. Culturally it would have been frowned upon for the lady to take the first step – I could just imagine somebody telling me one day that, "After all, you were so desperate that you went chasing after the man"! My contacting him would also have deprived me of the joy of being sought-after. But I happily gave my number and hoped that it would not be long before the first phone call came through.

All too soon, we were back in London, and it was time for me to say goodbye to Sam.

"Make sure that you keep me informed of how things develop between you and my friend," he teased me before we parted company. "I'm sure you will both get on," he added.

I promised to do that, gave him a big hug and went in search of my girlfriends; we had lots of things to discuss!

Beyond the Shame

Pearls of Life

Blessed are they that dwell in thy house: they will be still praising thee.

Psalm 84:4

And it came to pass, when King Hezekiah heard it, that he rent his clothes, and covered himself with sackcloth, and went into the house of the Lord.

Isaiah 37:1

And he came to Nazareth, where he had been brought up: and as his custom was, he went into the synagogue on the Sabbath day, and stood up for to read.

Luke 4:16

And they were continually in the temple, praising and blessing God. Amen.

Luke 24:52

2

GOD'S FAITHFULNESS OVER THE YEARS

Faithful is He that calleth you, who also will do it.

1 Thessalonians 5:24

In the quiet of my room, I thanked God profusely for His mercies and grace. I thanked Him for His faithfulness, how good He has been, how good He is and how good He would always be.

My worship of Him took on a whole new meaning. *What have I done*, I prayed, *to deserve such favour from You?*

As I looked back over the years – four years of enjoying and desiring growth in the things of the Lord – I was overwhelmed by God's faithfulness; I felt so much at peace (Phil 4:7: "And the peace of God which passeth all understanding, shall keep your hearts and minds through Christ Jesus"). I knew without a shadow of doubt that whatever happened in the future, God's will would be done in my life if I allowed it – that is, if I did not attempt to "help" God because things were going too slowly or not the way I wanted them to go.

God's Grace and Love

The road ahead may be difficult. It may be lonely, dark and slippery. It may seem as though everything else was falling apart. But so long as I remained focused on God, I would make it. I would endure the difficult and narrow path because I chose to place absolute trust in Him.

The victory would not have been the fact that I did not suffer shame, scorn, sorrow or pain, but that through it all I found strength by the grace of God to hold on to His promises (Jer 1:12: "Then said the

Lord unto me, thou has well seen: for I will hasten my word to perform it").

Through God, I found strength and grace to remain in the church He had planted me in, even as I looked around and realized that I seemed to be lagging behind in terms of the natural things we had all prayed about so long ago.

I found refuge in God's love, and I found a hiding place in the teachings that I received from my pastor. I am so thankful, for without this, I would definitely have given up in defeat (Jer 3:15: "And I will give you pastors according to mine heart, which shall feed you with knowledge and understanding").

I also discovered again and again, God's forgiving nature and His mercies – for in times when I considered veering off, He looked at me with eyes of compassion and reminded me that His grace is sufficient for me (2Cor 12:9: "And he said unto me, My grace is sufficient for thee; for my strength is made perfect in weakness. Most gladly therefore will I rather glory in my infirmities, that the power of Christ may rest upon me").

And guess what. Some of that compassion is rubbing off on me. I don't see life in black and white anymore. I am not so eager to jump to conclusions, and I find that I am so easily drawn to weak and imperfect individuals.

When I look at people, I wonder what their stories are. I wonder what I can do to encourage them and what help I can give. I want to tell them of the love of God; I want to encourage them that all is well. I want to reassure them that God will make a way for them and that there is a reason for whatever they're going through. In the end, God's specific purpose for their lives will be revealed if they do not give up in despair.

All is not lost, I say to anyone that I have the opportunity to do so. I am able to say to them repeatedly that God will honour them if they do not give up (Psa 3:3: "But thou, O Lord, art a shield for me; my glory and the lifter up of mine head").

Holding On

As the years have gone by, I have been so grateful to God for the refreshing times of prayer I had. Those times have helped me stand

(Eph 6:13: "Wherefore take unto you the whole armour of God, that ye may be able to withstand in the evil day, and having done all, to stand"). They helped me keep on believing when the only option seemed to give up and move on to other things.

There were times my flesh betrayed me; I found that I was attracted to some pleasant non-Christians. I was faced with the choice of holding on to the truths of the Christian upbringing I had believed in, or of looking around and making a decision based on my own circumstances. But for the grace and mercy of God, I would not have been able to walk away.

My times of prayer helped me to say no when I was five, eight, and nine years younger than I am now, to marriage proposals from both pleasant unbelievers and nice Christians who felt that it was enough to know Jesus as Lord but that anything more was being too fanatical. These were people I knew would divert me from the call of the Lord upon my life.

Those were difficult times, difficult seasons, when I looked at what appeared to be very good opportunities of marriage, but I had to gather my inner strength, overcome my fears of missing a marriage opportunity and say no, because I was trying to put what God required of me before my own desires.

I believe those times spent in prayer also helped me to overlook the eyes of scorn. You can feel it when the disdain of others is directed toward you, and it is real – and sometimes, unfortunately, not just from unbelievers.

Those prayer times also gave me strength to say no and just to think about the fact that I would cause Jesus pain by giving in to my own physical needs and desires.

Much to my surprise, the sudden desire I felt for the opposite sex was much stronger in recent years than when I did not know so much about the things of God. That was strange; for it seemed as though the stronger I grew in Christ, and the more I learnt about the things of God and increased in spiritual responsibility, the more these desires began to creep up on me. It was a humbling time, for as an unbeliever I had not struggled with this, these thoughts of sexual desire.

I yearned to talk about this, but I was no longer a baby Christian; I was actually teaching others about walking holy (Eph 4:1: "I therefore, the prisoner of the Lord, beseech you that ye walk worthy of the vocation wherewith ye are called").

I learnt again what I already knew about keeping the flesh under the spirit's control (1Cor 9:27: "But I keep under my body, and bring it into subjection: lest that by any means, when I have preached to others, I myself should be a castaway").

During this time I learnt that God is interested in building our characters. I learnt about the grace of God and how not to be judgmental. I began to be more compassionate towards others instead of concluding they had not been serious in the things of God because they veered off the straight and narrow path.

The Persistent Desire

I honestly believe I was storing up prayer accounts in spiritual banks which are now yielding interest in moments when I cannot pray.

Because, believe you me, the desire for marriage has not gone away. The desire to have a family of my own is as strong as ever, no matter how much I have tried to move it behind my spiritual activities, no matter how spiritual I have desired to be.

I have sometimes cried out to God in anguish, *Why don't You make this go away, so that I can get on with my life?* But the desire remains; it is still there. It is like a thorn in my flesh, this desire to marry a believer, which humbled me so much (2Cor 12:9: "And he said unto me, My grace is sufficient for thee: for My strength is made perfect in weakness").

I have sometimes felt like the woman with the issue of blood (Mark 5:25–29: "And a certain woman which had an issue of blood ... And straightway the fountain of her blood was dried up: and she felt in her body that she was healed of her plague"), although in my case I think that as much as I touched the hem of Jesus' garment, the issue of desiring to be married to a believer has not dried up! But maybe it is not supposed to.

The desire to marry has not gone away. If anything at all, I am even more aware of my hope to get married!

I have sometimes felt the need to apologize for this, though I did not put the desire there myself (Gen 2:18: "And the Lord God said, it is not good that the man should be alone; I will make him an help meet for him") – and this is emphasized later on in the New Testament (Hbr 13: 4: "Marriage is honourable in all").

If I had any control over this desire, I would get rid of it immediately so I would not have to deal with what had become a burden – so no one will see my need, my Achilles heel.

Pearls of Life

Know therefore that the Lord thy God, he is God, the faithful God, which keepeth covenant and mercy with them that love him and keep his commandments to a thousand generations.

Deuteronomy 7:9

Thy mercy, O Lord, is in the heavens; and thy faithfulness reacheth unto the clouds.

Psalm 36:5

I will sing of the mercies of the Lord forever; with my mouth will I make known thy faithfulness in all generations.

Psalm 89:1

Let us hold fast the profession of our faith without wavering for; (for he is faithful that promised).

Hebrews 10:23

3

WAITING EAGERLY FOR THE PHONE CALL

But if we hope for that we see not, then do we with patience wait for it.

Romans 8: 25

I waited eagerly for the phone call that could change my life's direction. I was excited; it seemed that, at long last, a genuine Christian man was going to look my way.

I felt as though not only had God answered my prayers – it seemed he had given me the cream of eligible Christian bachelors: not just a believing brother in the Lord but someone who, in addition to believing in the things of God, had taken a step further to involve himself in the work of the ministry, somebody working for the Lord.

And for my own selfish reasons at the time, I knew that being in a relationship with a more spiritual person would also enable me to excel or at least encourage me to get more involved in the things of God. I would have no choice but become more anointed due to my association with him.

I called my friend Ruth in Ghana to update her on recent happenings and to find out how much she knew about the man in question. It turned out that, indeed, she knew David; he had been in high school with her husband.

One thing I remember her saying clearly was that David was a faithful person, somebody who dearly loved the Lord. However, she asked me not to get too excited, as there had been no contact between either of us as yet.

"You know something, Emefa?" she said. "He might not like you in that way, and I don't think he will follow through just because there has been an introduction – so guard your heart and don't start planning things yet. I know you have been waiting a long time to do just that – but no wedding catalogues yet!"

I sensed the smile in her voice even as she said that. Ruth could play the devil's advocate, due to our longstanding relationship over the years. She was more of a sister than a friend, and she felt comfortable speaking her mind in truth and in love.

"Honestly, Ruth, can't a girl dream?" I reasoned with her. "It's just like you to bring me down to earth with a big thud."

"Of course I wouldn't want you to stop dreaming – in other words, living in hope," Ruth responded with a laugh. "But," she continued, "it is also wisdom to be aware of all the possible facts and prepare yourself for any eventuality – and not to leave church offended with Sam if things don't work out the way you want them to."

We chatted for a while longer, and I reminded her not to drop any hints to any member of my family yet; they would even get more excited than I was. God bless their hearts, but I wasn't yet ready for questions.

"Anyway," Ruth said just before we hung up, "desire and pray that you will be friends, because friendship is so important in any relationship that is going to last."

Still Expecting the Phone Call

As I waited for the phone call to come through, I wondered what my reaction would be if David did not call. Would I ask Sam for his number and contact him myself – or would that be seen as being too desperate? On the other hand, if I did not make an effort to call him, would it be seen as pride?

I decided that prayer was the way to handle this (Phil 4:6: "Be careful for nothing but in everything by prayer and supplication with thanksgiving let your requests be made known unto God").

I knew that, whether Sam's friend called or not, I would accept it as part of God's plan for my life, as part of the way that God wanted to lead me. But, of course, in my heart I knew that I would feel rejected if he made no attempt to start the process of getting to know me. Being a woman, that would have rankled a bit – female pride, you know.

It wasn't until after the end of that week that the expected phone call came through. I now know that David was also definitely making his own investigations.

In actual fact Ruth telephoned during the week and said that he had visited them – and without his appearing to be asking questions about me, my name had somehow come up in their conversations. And, of course, I had been Ruth's bridesmaid, so my pictures were prominently displayed in their albums.

Ungodly Advice from an Old Friend?

As I walked home from the train station after work at the end of that week, I thought again of a phone call I had had from an old school friend, Anita. She had been told that I no longer appeared to be without direction in my life. That is, I was now becoming quite serious in my walk with the Lord – and, according to reports, did not make much effort to spend time with old friends anymore.

"Are we no longer holy enough for you to spend time with, now that you are such a serious Christian?" she accused me, even as I expressed my delight at her call. "Anyway, Anita had continued after a while, "haven't you met anyone yet? How come you are still single? I am sure there must be lots of brothers at your church. Without waiting for an answer, she went on to tell me about the joys of married life, about her two wonderful children and the third on the way, and her just so wonderful and amazing husband.

Oh Lord, I prayed silently in my heart as she went on and on about the joys of marriage, *give me wisdom! May I not get upset, even though she is being so insensitive.*

Why do some people think that the good and faithful men are waiting on shelves and we just need to go shopping and pick up the ones we would like to take home? I wondered as my girlfriend continued her tirade. *Or why do some people conclude that* you *must be the reason why you are still not married at a certain age? You must be so picky and choosy when you are still without a ring on your finger. Don't blame me for not being married!* I cried within, *and do help me, God, not to respond in a manner unworthy of Your grace and love.*

Father, I continued to pray silently in my heart, *may I use this opportunity to glorify Your goodness and faithfulness. May my reaction not be one of the flesh, desiring to justify myself, but through the words that You give me may I enable her to see that Your ways are always the best for us* (Isa 55:8: "For my thoughts are not your thoughts, neither are your ways my ways, saith the Lord").

"Don't wait too long!" Anita cautioned me. "After all, you are not getting any younger – and if the person is not a serious Christian yet, or not a member of your church, surely after you get together you can change him! When I met my husband, he was not a committed Christian, but now with much fasting and prayer, he is gradually getting more committed, and he even leads the prayer meetings in church."

Anita hardly paused for breath but continued before I could get a word in. "I have rather become a bit more laid back. So get your act together, girl! God helps those who help themselves."

"My dear Anita," I was able to answer her with a smile in my voice, "just tell me where in the Bible to find the words you just quoted. I can rather remember a verse which encourages us to depend on God for all that we desire." (Psa 37:4: "Delight thyself also in the Lord: and he shall give thee the desires of thine heart.")

"Anyway" I continued, knowing that she would be interested in a bit of harmless chit-chat, "I may soon have news for you in that area, but you will have to wait a bit longer before I spill the beans."

"Oh come on, Emefa," Anita tried to get me talking. "Stop being so secretive! Have you met someone in your church? That has always been what you wanted anyway."

No amount of persuasion could get me talking, though, and after a few more minutes, she bade me goodbye with a promise to keep in touch more regularly.

Whew! I said to myself when I hung up the phone. *I could easily have lost my peace when she started talking about marriage and my single state. Thank God for His grace!*

The Phone Call

By the time I got home, I had relegated all thoughts of Anita and her endless questions and counsel to the back of my mind. It had been an extremely tiring day at work that day, and I was looking forward to a quiet evening at home, preparing for a meeting at church the next day.

I was soon so engrossed in the book I was reading – *Lay People and the Ministry*, by Dag Heward-Mills – that the shrill ringing of the phone an hour or two later completely took me surprise.

"Hello?" I said as I picked up the phone absentmindedly. I had just got to a very interesting part of the book, and I was fully absorbing the truths of what I was reading.

"Hello," answered someone whose voice I didn't recognize. It was a man, and he asked to speak with me.

"Emefa speaking," I responded, noting even then that the caller appeared to have a very nice, cultured voice.

It turned out to be the phone call I had been expecting for the past few days, from David. I can still remember sitting upright all of a sudden and straightening my skirt and patting my hair, almost as though he could see me through the phone. I had this absurd feeling that I had to look very presentable. Oh, how anxiety can sometimes cause us to behave in funny ways!

Even after all these years, I remember thinking that he had a nice baritone voice and spoke so clearly and confidently. I am sure it must have had something to do with his leadership training.

My first impression was that he seemed very pleasant. I did my best to overcome my own feelings of awkwardness and shyness, and tried to be pleasant and easy to talk to as well.

He asked me about church – I am sure that was an ice breaker tool. Whether I was enjoying it and what decisions I had made as a result of the recent camp meeting.

By the time we finished chatting, we both realized we had a few more friends in common and, interestingly, a few of them went to the same church I attended.

David promised to call again in the next few days and asked me to extend his regards to my pastor here in London, as well as to Yvette and her sister Rachel. I think he wanted to be seen as a serious suitor right from the beginning, not as someone with ulterior motives.

As soon as I put the phone down, I called my friend Ruth. I needed to give her the latest information.

"Ruth!" I nearly screamed down the phone line. The whole of Accra must have heard me! "Guess what! David called, and he seemed so nice!"

"But why are you so surprised?" Ruth replied. "I told you he was a nice person. And moreover he is a serious Christian. He would certainly know what to say to put you at ease.

"So between you and me," she continued, "would you like him to call again? You know I won't hold you to your words at this time."

"I think so," I answered truthfully. "We were able to chat for a while, and I would like to get to know him better."

After chatting for a few minutes, Ruth and I said our goodbyes, and I promised to keep her updated on any new developments.

I picked up the phone again and called my other friend, Yvette. I wasted no time in telling her about the phone call. She was so pleased for me and assured me that David was a nice and faithful brother who would not mess around with anyone.

Pearls of Life

Rest in the Lord, and wait patiently for him; fret not thyself because of him who prospereth in his way, because of the man who bringeth wicked devices to pass.

Psalm 37:7

The Lord is good to unto them that wait for him, to the soul that seeketh him.

Lamentations 3:25

For the vision is yet for an appointed time, but at the end it shall speak and not lie; though it tarry, wait for it; because it will surely come, it will not tarry.

Habakkuk 2:3

But let patience have her perfect work, that ye may be perfect and entire, wanting nothing.

James 1:4

4

A FRIENDSHIP BEGINS TO DEVELOP

Be ye not unequally yoked together with unbelievers: for what fellowship hath righteousness with unrighteousness? and what communion hath light with darkness?

2 Corinthians 6:14

So David and I began a friendship across the miles. I telephoned Sam to let him know that his friend and I seemed to be getting on quite well.

My friends teased me endlessly.

"Emefa," Yvette laughed, "these days your phone seems to be constantly engaged! Is it working at all?"

"I think," her husband Bernard put in, "she must have been following up on the new people who came to church on Sunday. But then," he added, with a twinkle in his eyes, "I am sure you had time to make a few personal calls to Accra also, for 'all work and no play' is not pleasing unto the Lord. Everybody needs a balance in life and this is your season, sister!"

Benefits of a Godly Association

In addition to a friendship developing, I was also continually being encouraged about working for the Lord. I remember how David guided me, on a few occasions, on how to prepare and share on some topics at our weekly meetings. So not only was I getting guidance from my pastor in church, but this friendship was also proving invaluable, in that I was getting good counsel and advice about handling my teaching group as well.

A friendship begins to develop

David reminded me all the time of the blessing of being given the opportunity to be involved in the ministry of the Lord (Psa 65:4: "Blessed is the man whom thou choosest, and causest to approach unto thee, that he may dwell in thy courts: we shall be satisfied with the goodness of thy house, even of thy holy temple").

A few weeks after we had started communicating, my friend David sent me pictures of himself, and I also did the same – though he had had the advantage of having already seen my pictures at Ruth's.

By the time David's pictures arrived, I had settled with God and myself that I would be led by the spirit and not be carnal (Rom 8:14: "For as many as are led by the by the Spirit of God, they are the sons of God"). Whereas in the past I had been led by particular expectations, this time I was determined to be spiritual about my decisions.

I am sure other Christian girls like me, if they are honest, would admit to having had certain expectations about would-be suitors. We have all grown up with certain ideas; we hope to meet somebody in the course of life's journey, fall in love and get married. The man we meet would be perfect in every way, even though we ourselves, have lots of imperfections. This gentleman would be our own special Prince Charming, come to rescue us from some unhappy situation, and all other things would fall into place, and we would then live happily ever after.

Blame it on all the fairy stories most of us read as children – the "They lived happily after" stories. Some people grow out of them quickly, but others, like me, had spent a bit more time romanticizing the whole idea of the relationship between men and women.

By this time, I was aware that I had to grow out of those absurd ideas and allow myself to be led by the sprit of God and not by storybook ideas of suitable marriage partners.

Church Life

Meanwhile church life was going on pretty well. We were learning more and more about how to be labourers for the Lord. It was a joy to go on outreaches, evangelise and tell people about Jesus Christ, and also to follow up on invitations made to people to come to church.

In the midst of this, I held close to my heart the possibility of a relationship to end all questions of "Who will ask me out? Who will seek that special relationship with me?"

Apart from my inner circle of very close friends, however, I hadn't gone about telling all and sundry about the possibility of a relationship between me and David. It was still early days, and moreover it was really wisdom to wait till something definite had been established.

I remember I had a chat with my pastor. I was so full of joy and hope that I giggled throughout our conversation. My pastor advised me that, as David and I seemed to be getting along so well, we should consider meeting up soon; it was important for us to meet in person and take matters from there.

Going Home

Going home to Ghana for a holiday wasn't part of my plans then; I simply could not afford it. But God being so good, my father offered to buy a ticket for me to come home at Christmas time that year. It was his sixtieth birthday, and he wanted me to be part of the celebrations.

Whoa! Thus David and I overcame the hurdle of how to meet, and I began to make plans for going to Ghana. David was also pleased; everything seemed to be working out so well. David and I had now been communicating for about four and half months.

My family and friends were also looking forward eagerly to my visit to Ghana. Ruth had made a list of friends I definitely had to see whilst I was there. My baby sister Kafui's list of items that she needed from London seemed to be getting longer and longer as my departure time drew nearer, but my suitcases were already packed, and I was determined not to rush out panic-buying this time.

At last, the long-awaited day was in sight; it was the evening of my departure to Ghana.

I prayed to God that night. I prayed that I would always be pleasing to Him. I prayed that He would order my steps. I prayed for wisdom (James 1:5: "If any of you lack wisdom, let him ask of God, that, giveth to all men liberally, and upbraideth not; and it shall be given him").

In my mind, I had gone over and over the first words of greeting when David and I would finally meet in person. Would I shake hands with him and say, "Hello, how nice to finally meet you"? Or would we hug spontaneously and just carry on from there?

A friendship begins to develop

The journey went very smoothly, and barely six hours after leaving the UK, my plane arrived in Accra, Ghana.

It was good to be back home, and everyone was excited that it had been possible for me to make it for my father's birthday party. My father did not have any idea that by enabling me to be in Accra, he had also made it possible for me to meet David.

Family Expectations

As usual, my mother and siblings were anxious to find out whether I had met somebody special in England. My mother was particularly anxious, as she felt I might not have been thinking seriously enough about marriage at that time. She would have dearly loved to have married me off as soon as she could, if she'd had the power to do so. Added to this were her not-so-subtle hints about my having children and how she needed to be full of strength herself in order to enjoy the role of a grandmother.

Over and over she would say things to me like "I do so wish you could marry soon and give me grandchildren whilst I have life, first of all, and also the energy to play with them."

I remember a conversation about marriage and having children that my sister Jiffa and I had had with my mother on a previous visit home in 1998.

"Emefa," my mother had said to me, very anxiously, "you need to think seriously about marriage and bearing children, in addition to your desire to be a serious Christian. As a woman, there really is a time span within which you can have children."

"Mama dear," I responded jovially, in an attempt to lighten the atmosphere, "you will be such a sweet grandma! You can even help me choose some names now, for all the four babies the Lord is going to bless me with."

Jiffa turned to look at me in surprise, as if to say, *You can't be serious! You really mean four children, in these times?*

"Anyway, Mama Grace," Jiffa said teasingly, "Sarah was ninety years when she had a child. Have faith."

My mother shook her head in exasperation at us both. "Are you Sarah?" she retorted. "Moreover, remember that faith without works is dead – and I don't seem to see your sister making much of an effort."

I gave my mother a hug and subtly changed the topic.

My maternal grandmother, Victoria – bless her heart – also badly wanted great-grandchildren. According to her, my mother, as her only child, had disobeyed her by only having four children! It was clear that she was all set out to do battle for more children in the family! It was therefore our generation's responsibility, starting with myself as the first child, to do what my mother had not done.

Oh dear, the pressure was on from all angles. However, it was not so bad this time, as a lot of attention was being focused on getting everything right for my father's birthday celebrations.

"There's someone on the phone for you," Jiffa called out to me later in the evening of my first day back home.

I guessed it would be David, and it was. Being the thoughtful person that he was, he had allowed for the fact that I needed to spend the first few hours chatting with my family and getting all the family news before he should try to get in touch with me.

"Welcome home again, Emefa. How was your journey?" David asked when I picked up the phone.

"It's amazing, David," I told him. "The journey did not seem so long this time. I don't normally sleep soundly when travelling, but this time I guess I was just so tired that I spent most of the journey asleep. I was pleasantly surprised when I woke up and realised we would be arriving in Accra in less than an hour's time."

"Well", David said, with a smile in his voice, "it's so great that you are here in Ghana. We have been expecting you."

We chatted for a while longer and arranged for him to come by the house the next day. I made a few more phone calls myself that evening, to Ruth and to a couple of my aunts – then fell into bed exhausted. It had been a long day!

A friendship begins to develop

Pearls of Life

A friend loveth at all times, and a brother is born for adversity.

Proverbs 17:17

A man that hath friends must show himself friendly: and there is a friend that sticketh closer than a brother.

Proverbs 18:24

Iron sharpeneth iron; so a man sharpeneth the countenance of his friends.

Proverbs 27:17

Henceforth I call you not servants; for the servant knoweth not what his Lord doeth; but I have called you friends; for all things that I have heard of my father I have made known unto you.

John 15:15

5

A MARRIAGE PROPOSAL

And the Lord God said, It is not good that the man should be alone; I will make him an help meet for him.

Genesis 2:18

I woke up quite early the next day. The sun's rays filtered through the curtains into my bedroom. I heard the sound of a cock crowing in the distance and the birds beginning their medley of songs as a new day began to break forth again.

Quiet Time

I turned around and reached for my Bible, just by my bedside. I treasured this time of the day, when, in the quietness and stillness of the early morning, I could embrace God's presence and just enjoy being at one with Him. I would cry out to Him for wisdom and grace, even as I thanked Him for His daily mercies towards me.

I brought the growing friendship between David and me before the Lord again and prayed that His will for both of us would come to pass in our lives (Eph 6:6: "Not with eyeservice, as men-pleasers; but as the servants of Christ, doing the will of God from the Heart"; Psa 143:10: "Teach me to do thy will; for thou art my God: thy spirit is good; lead me into the land of uprightness").

After some time in prayer, I stepped out of my room, ready to take in my stride what the day had to offer, and went in search of the rest of the family.

Family Joy

Our joy as a family that morning was complete, because just as we were about to have breakfast, my brother Lorlor, who had said it was impossible for him to make it to Ghana from the USA, gave us the greatest surprise of all when he turned up unannounced from the airport. Amidst much laughter and hugs all around, Lorlor explained that he had decided the best present he could give my father was to turn up in Ghana.

"So, big sis," Lorlor said to me, "are you still available for introduction to a Christian brother? I have got quite a few people I'd like to talk to you about."

"Hey, Lorlor," I answered, playfully pulling at his ears, "none of your cheek, young man – I am sorted."

That, of course, got everyone quiet, awaiting further explanations from me.

"Don't worry," I said to them. "You will know soon enough, and God will not disappoint you." That was all I would say.

"That's so cool," Kafui could not help chipping in, with a mischievous glint in her eyes. "That, of course, means that as one of your bridesmaids-to-be, I will also get to have some new dresses and shoes."

Honestly, I thought to myself with a smile, *there only has to be a hint of somebody around me and everyone starts thinking of a wedding!*

David, My Friend

David came to the house later that morning.

I felt I already knew him because we had been chatting on the phone for a while now and we had seen each other's pictures. On the other hand, it had all the awkwardness that one might expect from a first meeting.

After the initial pleasantries, we chatted easily for a while and caught up on each other's news. The real test of whether David and I were suited for one another in terms of marriage would be answered after we had spent a few days in each other's company.

And that's what we did for the next few days. We tried as much as possible to spend a lot of time together, getting to know each other better.

It was great to explore the sights of Accra again with David. A lot of very nice restaurants had sprung up in the time that I had been away.

We also went to the beach to pray. That was one of my best memories of those times. I had never been to the beach to pray before, and the experience was so awesome. I felt at one with nature and with God. My spirit was still before the greatness of the Almighty Lord, and as I lifted up my eyes towards heaven, I couldn't help but be grateful for God's interest in me, a mere mortal (Psa 8:4: "What is man, that thou art mindful of him? and the son of man, that thou visitest him?").

We spent time in David's church and mine. We visited each other's homes and met each other's siblings and friends. My siblings could not stop teasing me.

We enjoyed each other's company and had several discussions about living holy and striving to be a Christian and a labourer in the house of the Lord (Eph 4:11–12: "And he gave some, apostles; and some, prophets; and some, evangelists; and some, pastors and teachers; For the perfecting of the saints, for the work of the ministry, for the edifying of the body of Christ").

I admired how David worshipped God in song and in prayer. I realized he had absolute control over the people he was leading to and establishing in Christ. David communicated well with them and was able to get them to understand very easily the truths of God's word that he was trying to teach them.[1] They obeyed his instructions eagerly and looked to him for guidance – and David always seemed to have the exact words to calm their anxieties, compassion enough to draw out their fears, and wisdom to answer their questions.

My Doubts

Somewhere along the way, I began to feel that though the spiritual aspect of our relationship seemed to be growing in leaps and bounds, I was not too sure about the personal aspect, the boy/girl

---

[1] Dag Heward-Mills, *The Art of Leadership*, 175–176.

relationship factor. I began to feel that perhaps David and I were best suited only for friendship and not as marriage partners.

However, I decided to give the relationship more time and offer it to God, as I was very confused. I did not want to be counted amongst those who had rejected good men – but at the same time, I desperately needed to have the peace of God, for that is what tells us whether we are doing right, whenever we face any decision. (Col 2:15: "and let the peace of God rule in your hearts").

I may unconsciously have sent out a signal for help in making a truthful and spiritual decision concerning my relationship with David. To anyone who knew me well, I may have appeared rather subdued after having finally met someone who, to all intents and purposes, seemed to be ideal for me.

During this time, one of my senior pastors took me aside and spoke to me. He asked me to be truthful, to God and to myself.

"Do you really want to go ahead with this relationship?" he asked me in concern, with eyes full of compassion.

Alas, I could not be honest with him, because I thought of what people would say.

In hindsight, I suppose I wanted to be liked, I wanted to please a lot of people, so I continued to hope that I would feel the way I was supposed to feel (at peace with being in a relationship) – but I would go to bed confused and crying out to God for His direction.

I believe David could sense my confusion and the fact that I did not seem to be at peace. I had been home barely ten days, and already things were moving along quite fast. I tried to slow things down a bit so we would not rush into anything, nor let our emotions lead us to make certain decisions.

Will You Marry Me?

Towards the end of my second week at home, David asked me to marry him.

I looked at him and thought, *Why couldn't you have waited a while?* I had always imagined how I would react when I was proposed to. But although I had suspected that it seemed likely, I was unprepared for it at that particular time.

Instead of joy, I felt sadness in my heart, for I loved and liked David as a brother, as a friend and as a fellow believer in the Lord. But my feelings were not the kind one would expect to experience towards a future husband. I didn't know if I could give him the kind of love, he needed to have from me in the future, the love he deserved to have from a future spouse.

I know love grows; it can start from nothing and become something great. But there are also different kinds of love – *agape, phileo, eros*[2] – and are they not each uniquely special? I didn't know if I could commit to love David as a wife should love a husband.

I usually try not to pretend, and at that point I wondered if I could truthfully, and with all honesty, commit to being a good wife, because that was David's ultimate desire.

Don't get me wrong; there's nothing special about me. In actual fact, I am often plagued by lots of insecurities. I am not so fickle-minded or proud as to reject someone based on flimsy reasons like nationality, colour, education, etc.

Why, oh God? my soul cried out in anguish. A proposal of marriage is supposed to be a joyful event in one's life, but I was plagued with doubts and fears, and I was unhappy.

Why are You putting me through this difficult time of decision-making? I asked God over and over again, *Why couldn't I have had a straightforward relationship, like everyone else?*

I began to appreciate that God's hand is indeed in every good thing, and that for a couple to meet and like one another is indeed a blessing from God. It is a miracle that many people stumble into without being aware of having received favour from God!

For some people, God had cleared all the obstacles before they even became aware of one another. Some women mistakenly think they have the husbands they have now because they prayed, fasted, abstained from evil – and hey, presto! The Lord rewarded them with a good man. They are blissfully unaware of the mighty miracle-working power of God in their relationship (1Cor 4:7: "For who maketh thee to differ from another? And what hast thou that thou didst not receive? Now if thou didst receive it why dost thou glory, as if thou hadst not received it?"). Their parents approved of their choices, they enjoy a good relationship with their in-laws, and the marriage is blessed with

---

[2] As we know, agape is unselfish love, the Christian ideal, and phileo is brotherly love. Eros is defined by Wikipedia as passionate love, with sensual desire and longing. It deals mostly with sexuality and an intimacy that people often crave.

children. But be reminded that God has been in the background working out this miracle in detail.

At that time, I felt so burdened and guilty because of these feelings. I felt I was rejecting the affection and love of a good man.

But as the years have gone by I have also been rejected by good and nice Christian brothers whom I would have liked to get to know better and, if possible, enter into a relationship with. It seemed that both these Christian brothers and I were interested not only in being nice Christians, but also in working for the Lord. But, apparently, that alone may not be enough to guarantee a relationship leading to marriage

In the spiritual, it is possible that these men and I would have complimented each other's ministry to the Lord by the grace of God, as we were both of the same mind (Phil 1:27: "Only let your conversation be as it becometh the gospel of Christ: that whether I come and see you, or else be absent, I may hear of your affairs, that ye stand fast in one spirit, with one mind striving together for the faith of the gospel"). But the choice was not only mine; it takes two agreeable minds. These gallant soldiers of Christ have gone on to make their own choices.

At the time it happened, I felt the pain of rejection so deeply. It was a deep, raw wound. I felt so unworthy. I despaired of ever being accepted.

What is wrong with me? I had cried out to God. *Am I too fat? Am I too skinny? Am I too quiet? Do I talk too much? Is it because of my glasses? Am I too dark? What exactly is it, Lord?* I cried out to heaven.

There was no answer then. There was just a niggling suspicion at the back of my mind that perhaps it was a punishment from the Lord for my own rejection of David – though I had prayed about my final decision. I have since been able to clearly see that God is a God of compassion; He does not bear grudges and is not malicious. God is not out to get you for something you did.

It turns out that it is not personal. You are either attracted to someone or not; you either have deep feelings for one particular Christian sister or brother, or not.

With regard to David and me, my close friends could tell that I was battling with a decision. I was torn between a natural tendency to be truthful and a desire not to hurt anyone and to be acceptable and pleasing to all.

I could pretend and make everyone happy and pleased with me, or I could tell the truth and face the consequences. Alienation perhaps? (Gal 1:10: "For do I now persuade men, or God? Or do I seek to please men? For if I yet pleased men, I should not be the servant of Christ.")

I tried to be compassionate in my rejection of David's proposal, because I genuinely cared for him and wanted him to see that it would be better for us to remain good friends. Nonetheless, I said no to him.

But he convinced me that it could work and we should give it a try. I reconsidered because I genuinely did not want to hurt him – and because I really thought that perhaps I needed to cross another barrier of unspirituality.

No one could decide for me. Ruth would not say anything. Neither would Jiffa, nor any of my pastor friends. I remember so clearly, several years after, that everyone said the ultimate decision had been mine. I needed to cross that river by myself.

So I left back for London, having agreed to be in a relationship – and even more than that, having accepted David's marriage proposal.

Before I left, I told my parents about the developments and about the proposal.

"Well," my father said, "you know how we have always emphasized the fact that marriage is a blessing from God, Emefa. But you know, as your parents, it's now up to us to consider what you have told us in terms of a specific relationship between you and David. And I am sure that David's parents will also do the same regarding you."

My mother, who knows me so well, looked at me carefully and said, "You are rather subdued for someone who has just been proposed to. Surely, Emefa, you should be laughing and making excited phone calls to your friends all around. We have prayed over and over for this time in your life," she said. "Are you very sure this is your heart's desire?"

"I am very sure," I replied. I didn't want to discuss the matter any further.

A Marriage Proposal

Pearls of Life

Whoso findeth a wife findeth a good thing, and obtaineth favour of the Lord.

Proverbs 18:22

Two are better than one; because they have a good reward for their labour. For if they fall, the one will lift up his fellow: but woe to him that is alone when he falleth; for he hath not another to help him up.

Ecclesiastes 4:9–10

Nevertheless, to avoid fornication, let every man have his own wife, and let every woman have her own husband.

1 Corinthians 7: 2

But if they cannot contain, It is better to marry than to burn.

1 Corinthians 7:9

Marriage is honourable in all, and the bed undefiled.

Hebrews 13:4

6

STRIVING FOR GODLY PEACE

The Lord will give strength unto his people; the Lord will bless his people with peace.

Psalm 29:11

As I sat on the plane back to London, I considered all that had transpired during my visit home. God seemed to have answered my prayers concerning marriage in a different way than I had expected. However, I decided that my mind was made up; if it was the will of God, I would go ahead with it, even though my instinct was still that I should have stuck with my first answer.

I had done the required groundwork for a successful marriage in the sight of God. I had listened to godly counsel, so, I tried to tell myself, surely whatever I was feeling was just a figment of my own imagination or emotions, which I should not depend upon.

An Aspiring Wife – A Wife-in-Waiting?

My friends in London were happy for me, because I had found someone. I was now in a relationship with a Christian. I had kept the faith until then (2Tim 4:7: "I have fought a good fight, I have finished my course, I have kept the faith") and had not, out of desperation and the desire to marry at all costs, gone into a relationship with someone who did not hold dear the values that we had found in Christ. I was a serious and committed Christian's wife-in-waiting, a dear position of honour and esteem – and, of course, the less obvious matter of great *sacrifice!*

My secret was safe; no one would know of my indecision regarding the relationship. I mentioned to my pastor how it had all come about and the fact that despite my initial misgivings, I had made up my mind and was thus going ahead with the relationship.

Being single can be challenging; being a single Christian woman looking forward to marriage is not easy. After striving to live a life pleasing to God, you sometimes need to defend the stand you have taken to people who question your lifestyle.

In addition to this, I guess after Christians have encouraged you for a few years, they also might find it difficult to keep on encouraging you. People have their own struggles, and there are other problems requiring solutions. In order for people to handle their own issues in life, your needs may have to be relegated to the background. That's the way it is, and you need to develop the ability to handle this, hold on and press on.

Several people's attitude towards me changed; it was almost as though I had become very acceptable in the eyes of some of them because I was also in a relationship now. Some people were exceptionally nice – and I was grateful for that vote of confidence in me – because they had heard that David, was a truly gifted and faithful servant of the Lord. It was almost as though my value as a person had risen because I was now in a relationship.

My own confidence level also shot up. *Wow*, I reasoned with myself, *David's friends will become my friends. It will really be nice to be married to this great man of God. I will always have a front-row seat – will be ushered to this seat, especially during Church programmes. I will be respected and loved.*

I realized that a lot of good things would be happening to me. I would certainly benefit a lot from being married to a serious and committed Christian.

So the relationship continued over a period of almost a year. I was determined to be very spiritual about this relationship and pushed all doubts to the back of my mind.

However, my doubts would not go away. I really did not have the peace of God. I now realize that I must have behaved oddly, sometimes, for someone who was looking forward to marriage – because, basically, I was not at peace within.

Turning Point

Meanwhile David and I continued our relationship. Eventually, my father telephoned to discuss my proposed marriage.

He said that both he and my mother felt I didn't know my suitor well enough, and that we both seemed to be in a hurry to marry. They both felt – and I don't blame them in any way regarding my ultimate decision and my current state today – that David might not have been the right person for me. But if that was what I was determined to do, my father told me, I could go ahead and do as I wanted to.

Later I reflected carefully on the conversation I'd had with my father. It was clear to me that although they had nothing against David, they were not exactly giving their blessings to this marriage.

I was concerned about that, and it compounded my doubts because, surely, this was supposed to be the time when parents give their blessings and encourage you to go ahead with your marriage plans. I needed them to clearly give us their blessings for this marriage.

So even though I was still doubtful about the marriage and without the peace of God, at that time I was still willing to go ahead to the next level of preparations for my marriage (dishonest of me, perhaps, but that was it), based on my parents' blessing.

My parents would not commit to saying more than, "If this is what you want, then maybe you should do it."

I remember that, a few years after this incident, in one of my depressed moments, dealing with feelings of dejection and rejection, I complained bitterly to my parents that if only they had been more supportive, the marriage would have gone on.

I blamed my parents for this and for the fact that I was still unmarried. It was indeed a time of pain and sorrow; I needed someone to offload this on, and normally when one is hurting, one also hurts the people closest to one. I lashed out at them angrily, I cried and shed many tears: I believed that my parents had been the cause of the decision that I finally made, because as an obedient child, I couldn't have gone ahead and married without their express blessings. (I was, of course, conveniently forgetting my own doubts and indecision regarding the marriage.)

Striving for Godly Peace

But as time went on and I found peace with the Lord, I have been able to see that, really, my situation was no fault of theirs – and who knows if it was all part of God's plan for my life? Perhaps I had to go through this for a reason (Rom 8:28: "And we know that all things work together for good to them that love God, to them who are the called according to his purpose").

The months flew by, until I had been in the relationship with David for almost a year. Meanwhile, David was making every effort to come over to visit me; it was not yet possible for me to go back home again. So I continued to pray a lot. I prayed for God to direct my path (Psa 119:105: "for the word of the Lord is a lamp unto my feet and a light unto my path").

I also continued to read as much as I could about marriage. I remember that one of the messages which touched my heart in church then, was the advice to marry a friend – and, in addition to that, to marry somebody that you were sure you loved. I understood this to mean that there had to be something *more in addition to the natural love* we felt for one another as Christian brothers and sisters in God's kingdom. This, of course, led to more soul-searching on my part. David seemed to be at peace with everything; I was the one who was confused and unsure whether to go ahead or not.

Pearls of Life

Acquaint now thyself with him and be at peace: thereby good shall come unto thee.

Job 22:21

Thou wilt keep him in perfect peace, whose mind is stayed on thee: because he trusteth in thee.

Isaiah 26:3

Peace I leave with you, my peace I give unto you: not as the world giveth, give I unto you. Let not your heart be troubled, neither let it be afraid.

John 14:27

And let the peace of God rule in your hearts, to the which also ye are called in one body; and be ye thankful.

Colossians 3:15

7

THE DIFFICULT DECISION

The steps of a good man are ordered by the Lord: and he delighteth in his way.

Psalm 37:23

Eventually, after having been in the relationship with David for a year, I decided it was time for me to either get married despite my doubts, or to get out of the relationship. I had been praying for a year after the proposal, and it was time to act (James 2:17: "Even so faith, without works, is dead, being alone").

It came to the point that I knew I had to very honest with myself – or foolish, perhaps – and opt out of the relationship.

I knew that I would be walking a lonely road. I would be misunderstood; I might lose my friends; I might be labelled a proud person who had said no to a nice Christian man.

But I also knew that David and I couldn't continue in limbo; we had to either move on together in harmony or move on in different directions. I knew the cost of speaking the truth in love would be very high. I might be seen as a very foolish person, with my head in the clouds, still looking for the perfect person whilst not without imperfections myself.

David would never tell me he wanted out of the relationship, no matter how "badly" things were going or how I behaved. It was a matter of principle for him; he would be faithful to what he had started. As a Christian in leadership, it would not look well on his part to let me down after he had proposed to me – and, God bless his heart, I also know that he may also have sacrificed any doubts he had in order to protect me.

The Difficult Decision

The onus was then on me. Either I set David free in love, or I married him, thinking only of the possible benefits of being married to him. I chose to set him free.

A warm sense of God's love settled over me after I decided in my heart and my mind the course of action I was going to take. I felt secure in God's grace and in His arms, and a still small voice seemed to whisper, *You did the right thing – you prayed before you acted.* I felt the peace of God descend on me (Phil 4:7: "And the peace of God, which passeth all understanding, shall keep your hearts and minds in perfect peace").

I then told my pastor what I felt I had to do after much prayer and soul-searching, and out of the desire to do the right thing. I remember he advised me not to go into lengthy discussions over the issue with anyone. It wasn't necessary to do that; people would form their own opinions anyway, and there was no need to attempt to justify my actions.

That phone call towards the end of 2000, – the year of the millennium, the year of a new century, the year of much grace and hope – was one of the most painful and hurtful things I have ever had to do. I was going to cause someone pain, grief and sorrow – a good friend who had prayed with me, prayed for me and wished me well ever since we became acquainted.

Well, I made the phone call, and David was gracious; he released me from my promise to marry him. There were no accusations of having gone back on my word, there were no recriminations – there was only acceptance of my decision.

The next few days, though, were painful. There were lots of teary days, because I was afraid I would be misunderstood and rejected.

There were still days of confusion, when I would be plagued by thoughts that because of what I had done, nobody would want to be my friend. I was hurting inside, and one of my fears then was that, like the woman caught in adultery,[1] I might be seen as having committed an unpardonable sin – caught in the act of saying no to marriage.

---

[1] Jhn 8:3–11: "When Jesus had lifted up himself, and saw none but the woman, he said unto her, Woman, where are those thine accusers? Hath no man condemned

What if this story, I wondered sometimes, *is shared somewhere else and some people conclude that I am full of pride – somebody who says no to marriage proposals – and nobody ever offers me friendship leading to marriage?*

I also remember that one of my senior pastors happened to visit our church, and I had the opportunity of speaking with him. He asked me whether I had said no to the marriage because of my parents.

I thought carefully about his question. I knew that if I had been convinced that I should go ahead and marry David, I would have prayed for my parents to have a change of heart, as their blessing was so necessary and important. However, my final decision had been based on the fact that I did not feel able to marry David after I had prayed and fasted for a year.

So I replied that, though I needed to have my parents' blessing before going ahead with any marriage plans, in all honesty, I had already decided in my heart, after a year spent in prayer. I could not, therefore, blame my parents for the fact that the marriage had not taken place.

My senior pastor comforted me and said to me, "May God give you somebody that you love as a wife should love her husband" (Psa 84:11: "For the Lord God is a sun and shield: the Lord will give grace and glory: no good thing will he withhold from them that walk uprightly").

I have never forgotten those gracious words. They were like balm to my wounds (Jer 51:8: "take balm for her pain, if so be she may be healed").

---

thee? She said, No man, Lord. And Jesus said unto her, Neither do I condemn thee: go, and sin no more.

The Difficult Decision

Pearls of Life

But He knoweth the way that I take: when He hath tried me, I shall come forth as gold.

Job 23:10

Thou hast enlarged my steps under me, that my feet did not slip.

Psalm 18:36

He brought me up also out of an horrible pit, out of the miry clay, and set my feet upon a rock, and established my goings.

Psalm 40:2

Thy word is a lamp unto my feet and a light unto my path.

Psalm 119:105

Order my steps in the word: and let not iniquity have dominion over me

Psalm 119:133

8

BROKEN IN SPIRIT, YET DARING TO TRUST AGAIN

But our God is in the heavens, He has done whatsoever he hath pleased.

Psalm 115:3

It has been ten years since I made my decision, and a lot has happened since then. As I look back over the years, I realize that God has been so merciful. He has preserved my faith and trust in Him. The grace of God has enabled me to keep on walking and not to fall by the wayside.

I could easily have become a statistic. I could easily have rejected God's ways and ended up seeking to satisfy my own desires, even if it meant turning my back on God and His ways of leading us.

But now am so thankful for God's hand on my life. I am still here, by His grace.

Will I Marry?

I have wondered sometimes whether I will ever marry. I believe and pray so, for this precious daughter of God refuses to give up hope (Mark 11:22: "And Jesus answering saith unto them, Have faith in God").

But even if I do not get married, like the three Hebrew boys, Shadrach, Meshach and Abednego, at the court of Babylon,[1] I pray

---

[1] Daniel 3:17–18: "If it be so, our God whom we serve is able to deliver us from the burning fiery furnace, and he will deliver us out of thine hand O King. But if not, be it known unto thee, O King, that we will not serve thy gods, nor worship the golden image which thou has set up.

that I will not turn my back on my God who has loved me all these years. I pray that God, whom I love and serve, will deliver me from the hands of the enemy of our souls. So help me God!

I pray for grace to keep the faith, to continue believing in the ultimate faithfulness of God. I pray for the grace to keep believing in God's goodness, and through it all, I pray and desire to draw closer to God. I pray for strength to hold on and not to give up.

I sincerely believe that God will reward me for my years of believing in him (Psa 37:5: "Commit thy way unto the Lord; trust also in him; and he shall bring it to pass"). Do I regret that the years have gone by without the promise being fulfilled yet, in my youthful days when everything is a bit easier? Do I regret that unlike most of my friends I have no children yet? (Isa 54:1: "Sing Oh Barren, thou that didst not bear; break forth into singing, and cry aloud, thou that didst not travail with child: for more are the children of the desolate than the children of the married wife, saith the Lord.")

Sometimes in my low moments, I have wondered about some men I had genuinely liked, who had also liked me. As you know, there's no formula concerning the issues of the heart – so we guard it carefully (Pro 4:23: "keep thy heart with all diligence; for out of it are the issues of life"). I have wondered whether they might have become serious Christians if I had married them, regardless of the fact that when I first met them, going the extra mile in the things of God did not seem to be a priority for them.

Most of the time, however, I am grateful that the Lord has entrusted me with the privilege of trying Him at His word, the privilege of hoping in his faithfulness, for He is a faithful friend and father.

For, "What shall I render unto the Lord for all his benefits toward me?" (Psa 116:12). Indeed, the Lord watches over His word to perform it (Jer 1:12: "Then said the Lord unto me, Thou has well seen: for I will hasten my word to perform it").

The Passing Years

Sometimes I have felt the pain of the years passing by and the shame of still desiring something that seems so easy to get but which seemed somehow not to have been my portion yet – the shame of knowing that many people know or suspect that I want to get married.

Oh dear! (Psa 25:20–21: "Oh keep my soul, and deliver me: let me not be ashamed; for I put my trust in thee. Let integrity and uprightness preserve me; for I wait on thee.")

There have been moments when I have known that, but for the grace of God, I would have given up hope in the words of the Lord; I would not have continued in the faith. It was just too difficult to continue on this narrow path. But the grace of God enabled me not to give up in despair. (1Cor 10:23: "There hath no temptation taken you but such as is common to man: but God is faithful, who will not suffer you to be tempted above that ye are able; but will with the temptation also make a way to escape, that ye may be able to bear it.")

Along life's journey, I have met some good people, whom I had to gather strength to say no to, for anything more than a passing acquaintance. I went on certain seemingly harmless lunches and dinners out of the need for companionship – which I should have avoided, as they could easily have taken me off the path of God's best for me.

The realization of this made me even more aware that perhaps, unlike some, I had not been given the absolute grace of abstinence from the opposite sex, and as such was exposing myself to a lot of temptation toward a life which was not God's best for me (1Cor 7:2: "Nevertheless, to avoid fornication, let every man have his own wife, and let every woman have her own husband").

But I have also known the privilege of having been able to say no to some intimate relationships outside God's design for me, in spite of certain strong desires that I seemed to have. Initially, that made me proud, but I realized, as the years have gone by, that it was actually God's grace that delivered me from making certain mistakes.

A Broken Spirit

There have been times when feelings of anger and wrath overwhelmed me when I thought of David. I was angry because, as a result of a failed relationship with him, friends of David, and some friends of mine, would brand me as a heartbreaker – the lady who said no to him.

I felt – although I could have been wrong – that David had the support of our friends, as the person who had been rejected by the woman he wanted to marry, whilst I had struggled to come to terms with the way it had all transpired, on my own.

But I could not go around convincing everyone that my decision had not been an easy one despite the fact that I had prayed about it. I made my decision only after a lot of prayer – but I could not solicit understanding from our friends and onlookers, as to why I had come to that decision. There were questions I would have liked to have asked them – *Do you think it was easy for me to make that decision? Is the fact that we are both Christians enough for a lifetime commitment? Aren't there other factors, like temperament and compatibility, that could perhaps affect a lifetime decision between a man and a woman? Do emotions have no part to play in this?* I particularly wanted to find out from the married ones whether they got married based only on the fact that they both happened to be Christians.

Several times, I asked God whether He was trying to make me feel so rejected and ashamed that I would have no option but to leave the church. Feelings of frustration overwhelmed me, and my spirit was broken. I felt like a broken reed, struggling to maintain and sustain my faith in God, trying so hard to link the God of love with what I had gone through (Isa 42:3: "A bruised reed shall he not break, and the smoking flax shall he not quench: he shall bring forth judgement unto truth").

So many times, I felt like dying, disappearing off the face of the earth so people would be justified in saying, *Well, she said no, and now look at her end.*

I felt I was being referred to by some as the woman who had not married when she had the opportunity, and as a result was still not married. It seemed as though my punishment for not marrying David was to endure a prolonged season of shame!

It was a difficult time in my life, a lonely road, full of potholes, full of pain and grief. It felt like the valley of the shadow of death.

And to make matters worse for me, he got married, in a big wedding, and now has beautiful children! *Why, oh God, did You allow such a calamity to befall me?* I cried out to Him. *Why did You allow me to go through such humiliation? Why me?* I continued to question God.

I tried reasoning with the Almighty: *When I started serving You*, I cried out to Him, *You promised that I would have life and have it more abundantly* (Jhn 10:10: "The thief cometh not, but for to steal, and to kill, and to destroy: I am come that they might have life, and that they might have it more abundantly").

I trusted You, I screamed at God, with tears rolling down my cheeks. In the secret place of my room, I punched the bed in frustration; I broke a few items in anger at God, at Christians and at the world.

I continued to list all the ways in which I had obeyed God: *I have paid my tithe faithfully since I understood about paying tithe* (Mal 3:10: "Bring ye all the tithes into the storehouse, that there may be meat in mine house, and prove me now herewith, saith the Lord of hosts, if I will not open you the windows of heaven, and pour you out a blessing, that there shall not be room enough to receive it").

I have obeyed You, God, by honouring my parents – I love and respect them so much and do all I can to be a daughter who is pleasing to them (Eph 6:2–3: "Honour thy father and mother; which is the first commandment with promise; That it may be well with thee, and thou mayest live long on the earth).

I have obeyed You, God, by worshipping regularly in a local assembly. I am active in my church (Hbr 10:25: "Not forsaking the assembling of ourselves together, as the manner of is; but exhorting one another and so much the more as ye see the day approaching").

I have said no to possible marriage partners in order to be pleasing to You, I reminded God (2Cor 6:14: "Be ye not unequally yoked together with unbelievers: for what fellowship hath righteousness with unrighteousness? And what communion hath light with darkness?").

Oh Lord, I continued to cry out to Him, *is this how You reward those You have called to Yourself? Is this how You reward those seeking to serve You? Is this how You treat those who have chosen to trust You?* (Pro 3:5–6: "Trust in the Lord, with all your heart and lean not on your own understanding in all your ways acknowledge him and he shall direct your path.")

And the answer was silence… It was up to me to keep on trusting or to let go of what would be God's greatest gift to me, after salvation – trusting in His unfailing and eternal love for me! (Jer 31:3: "The Lord hath appeared of old unto me, saying, Yea, I have loved thee with an everlasting love: therefore with loving kindness have I drawn thee.")

Broken in Spirit, Yet Daring to Trust Again

As a result of this, I am convinced that the decision I made was the right one, and by the grace of God I did not make a mistake in not marrying David.

David was at that time, and is still, a fine anointed man serving the Lord with joy. I believe that, had our marriage been the will of God for us both, it would have come to pass.

The after-effects have been difficult and challenging, but that's sometimes the way things are when you take a stand for what you believe in.

Inevitably there would be some who would think I had made a mistake. It would not be my place to get them to think otherwise, but, rather, I ask their forgiveness for my mistake. Forgive me.

In addition to this, I would ask for further compassion for one who has made such a public mistake. Most of our mistakes are made in private, and a lot of people do not see them.

We are sometimes insensitive to those whom we think have made mistakes, and so we might drive them away from the very place where they should be comforted and loved. We need to be compassionate and gracious, as our Lord is (Rom 9:15: "For he saith to Moses, I will have mercy on whom I will have mercy, and I will have compassion on whom I will have compassion"; Mat 20:34: "So Jesus had compassion on them, and touched their eyes: and immediately their eyes received sight, and they followed him")

Pearls of Life

The Lord is nigh unto them that are of a broken heart; and saveth such as be of a contrite spirit.

Psalm 34:18

The sacrifices of God are a broken spirit: a broken and a contrite heart, O God, thou wilt not despise.

Psalm 51:17

He healeth the broken in heart, and bindeth up their wounds.

Psalm 147:3

Come, and let us return unto the lord: for hath torn, and he will heal us; he hath smitten, and he will bind us up.

Hosea 6:1

The Spirit of the Lord is upon me, because he hath anointed me to preach the gospel to the poor; he hath sent me to heal the broken hearted, to preach deliverance to the captives, and recovering of sight to the blind, to set at liberty them that are bruised.

Luke 4:18

9

THE HEALING RAIN OF GOD'S LOVE

The Lord hath appeared of old unto me, saying, Yea, I have loved thee with an everlasting love: therefore with loving kindness have I drawn thee.

Jeremiah 31:3

God is more interested in our character than in our comfort. I believe I am a much better person now; I am increasingly aware of God's grace and mercies towards me. God is still at work in me, daily instructing, directing, cleansing, encouraging, loving and purifying me, and doing all that needs to be done so that I may be totally pleasing to Him (Psa 138:8: "The Lord will perfect that which concerneth me: thy mercy, O Lord, endureth for ever: forsake not the works of thine own hands").

Balm of Gilead

I am humbled by God's tenderness – and above all, by the fact that He loves me so much. I am very confident of this now and know without a shadow of doubt that He will always give me the best for me.

He hurts when I hurt, especially when He sees my trust in Him wavering because I don't trust that He is working everything out for my good. God is taking my mess and giving me a miracle and a testimony, that somebody else may be healed, that somebody else may be comforted, that somebody else may know without a shadow of doubt that indeed our God is full of compassion.

God has not given up on us. His love for us is everlasting and is not dependent upon how good or perfect we have been.

I am learning to receive God's complete forgiveness and to believe that when He says He has forgiven me, He really has!

So can that be for you. Whatever you have been through, whatever you are going through, whatever you will go through – if indeed you have made the Lord Jesus lord of your life, there's no need to feel inferior, guilty or full of self-condemnation. Be free in the liberty that Jesus Christ died for you to have (Gal 5:1: "Stand fast therefore in the liberty wherewith Christ hath made us free, and be not entangled again with the yoke of bondage").

I am also learning to forgive over and over again as issues come up, and that positions me in the right place to receive more of God's grace.

As I spent time with the Lord, I realized I was full of unforgiveness, and a root of bitterness had taken hold of me (Hbr 12:15: "Looking diligently lest any man fail of the grace of God; lest any root of bitterness springing up trouble you, and thereby many be defiled"). Initially, I felt a lot of bitterness and anger towards my friend Sam and most of the people who knew both David and I.

Much of my anger was directed towards Sam, as he had started the process and I felt he had conveniently left the scene when there was trouble and I needed him as a friend. He was nowhere to be found, and I felt he had concluded that I was a proud person who should be left to suffer.

Honestly, who would not pray about such a serious issue as a marriage proposal? I wondered. *And who in their right mind would reject a good man based on flimsy excuses such as the colour of his skin, language, education, height or current residence?*

I gradually forgave Sam and others as time went on, as I learnt over and over again about the Lord's forgiveness of my own sins and how compassionate God is. In addition to this, I learnt again that in order to be pleasing to God, my heart had to be free of any grudges and unforgiveness towards anyone, so that my own prayers would not be hindered (Mark 11:25–26: "And when ye stand praying, forgive, if ye have ought against any: that your Father also which is in heaven may forgive you your trespasses. But if ye do not forgive, neither will your Father which is in heaven forgive your trespasses").

I recently met Sam at a retreat in Virginia, in the United States – and it was a time of genuine love, laughter and fellowship. We were able to laugh about his attempts at matchmaking, and he told me that after his botched attempt at fixing me up with his friend, he had retired from matchmaking. I encouraged him not to give up doing that; mine was just one of the ones that did not work out – and in any case, a little help by way of introducing people is a wonderful thing!

In the course of Christian activities, I have also met David again, and his lovely wife and their children. What could have been an awkward encounter the first time we met was rather a gracious meeting between fellow believers in the Lord!

Draw Me Near to Thee, Oh God!

All these experiences have enabled me to draw closer to God. I had no choice; humbled by all that was going on in my life, all I could do was to seek God more and more.

The rejection by man led naturally to a desperate search to find the Lord. I believe this has led to more grace on my life (James 4:6: "but he giveth more grace. Wherefore he saith, God resisteth the proud, but giveth grace unto the humble"). The grace to continue believing, grace to stay in the same environment – because I know myself: on my own, I would have gone seeking answers somewhere else, a definite getaway route for a proud person.

However, I want to know the Lord more and more; there is so much more to discover, and I know He has a lot more to do in my life. God is not finished with me yet (Phil 3:10: "That I may know him, and the power of his resurrection, and the fellowship of his sufferings, being made conformable unto his death"). I want to move forward and be all that God has called me to be, forgetting what lies behind and reaching forward to what lies ahead (Isa 43:18: "Remember ye not the former things, neither consider the things of old").

The time has come to let go of past hurts and offences, to stop blaming myself, to stop waiting for a sign from someone, for external validation that I have been forgiven and that it is well.

I extend the grace of God's mercy to you!

Isaiah 61:1–3

The spirit of the Lord God is upon me; because the Lord hath anointed me to preach good tidings unto the meek; he hath sent me to bind up the broken-hearted, to proclaim liberty to the captives, and the opening of the prison to them that are bound; to proclaim the acceptable year of the Lord, and the day of vengeance of our God; to comfort all that mourn; To appoint unto them that mourn in Zion, to give unto them beauty for ashes, the oil of joy for mourning, the garment of praise for the spirit of heaviness; that they might be called trees of righteousness, the planting of the Lord, that he might be glorified.

Pearls of Life

But God commended his love towards us, in that, while we were yet sinners, Christ died for us.

Romans 5:8

For I am persuaded that neither death nor life, nor angels, nor principalities, nor powers, nor things present, nor height, nor depth, nor any other creature, shall be able to separate us from the love of God, which is in Christ Jesus our Lord

Romans 8:38–39

Behold, what manner of love the father hath bestowed upon us, that we should be called the sons of God: therefore the world knoweth us not, because it knew him not.

1 John 3:1

And we have known and believed the love that God hath to us. God is love; and he that dwelleth in love dwelleth in God, and God in him.

1 John 4:16

10

NUGGETS OF GODLY WISDOM

For the hurt of the daughter of my people am I hurt; I am black; astonishment hath taken hold on, is there no balm in Gilead, is there no physician there? Why then is not the health of the daughter of my people recovered?

Jeremiah 8:21–22

For you, the woman who desires to marry and whom the Lord loves so passionately, our God is in heaven and He does whatsoever he pleases.

Don't doubt God's love. His love for you cannot be based on the challenges or trials you go through. Decide that you will hold on passionately to the love that God has shown you, before you even became aware of Him, for whilst we were yet sinners Christ died for us (Rom 5:8: "But God commended his love toward us, in that, while we were yet sinners, Christ died for us").

God's love for you is not based on whether you make the right or wrong choices. In fact, He has already said that He has forgiven us our sins and remembers them no more. Our sins have been thrown into the sea of forgetfulness, and in addition to this, His love for us – whether single (even through our own actions) or married – is everlasting (Jer 31:3: "The Lord hath appeared of old unto me, saying, Yea, I have loved thee with an everlasting love: therefore with loving kindness have I drawn thee").

Stepping Forward

It is time to pick yourself up and move on. The Lord wants to do a new thing in your life, but you may be hindering this by an obsession with what happened in the past (Isa 43:18–19: "Remember ye not the former things, neither consider the things of old. Behold, I will do a new thing; now it shall spring forth; shall ye not know it? I will even make a way in the wilderness, and rivers in the desert").

In order to move forward in God's plans for us, we must settle the matter once and for all. No more discussions about the rights and wrongs of a decision. It is time to bury all hurts, wounds, anger and offences related to your heartache, in order that the seeds of countless prayers prayed over you might germinate and bud (Jhn 12:24: "Verily, verily, I say unto you, Except a corn of wheat fall into the ground and die, it abideth alone: but if it die, it bringeth forth much fruit"), so that there might be new growth, so that you might be able to bear fruit as a Christian (Jhn 15:8: "Herein is my father glorified, that ye bear much fruit; so shall ye be my disciples").

Bear Fruits

Decide that you are tired of living below God's best for you. You could be a better minister of God's word. You could lead many more to righteousness if only you would stop focusing on what happened in the past. Remember Lot's wife? She died because she turned to look back: "But his wife looked back from behind him and she became a pillar of salt" (Gen 19:26).

There really is more to life than failed relationships. The Lord has so much more to offer you. It is also time to accept the Lord's forgiveness in everything – for if we say we have no sin, we deceive ourselves, but indeed, if you have made terrible mistakes, the Lord promises He does not keep a log book (Isa 43:25: "I, even I, I am he that blotteth out thy transgressions for mine own sake, and will not remember thy sins").

It is time to move forward and be all that God has called you to be, forgetting what lies behind and reaching forward to what lies ahead (Phil 3:13: "forgetting those things which are behind, and reaching forth unto those things which are before, I press toward the mark for the prize of the high calling of God in Christ Jesus").

Beyond the Shame

The Lord needs you to work in His vineyard, as a comforter, as an encourager, as a teacher of His word – as someone who is able to walk in victory so that others can also walk in Christ-given victory (Luke 22:31–32: "And the Lord said, Simon, Simon, behold, Satan hath desired to have you, that he may sift you as wheat: But I have prayed for thee, that thy faith fail not: and when thou art converted, strengthen thy brethren").

God is faithful, He is not a man, that He should lie. His purpose in all that is going on in your life is not to put you to shame (Psa 31:1: "In thee, O Lord, do I put my trust; let me never be ashamed: deliver me in thy righteousness"). He will complete the work He has begun in your life; He is a finisher of the work that He begins.

So rise up and surge forward! There is yet more land to conquer – and remember, it's all about pleasing Him!

Pearls of Life

So teach us to number our days that we might apply our hearts to wisdom.

Psalm 90:12

For the Lord giveth wisdom: out of his mouth cometh knowledge and understanding.

Proverbs 2:6

The fear of the Lord is the beginning of wisdom: and the knowledge of the holy is understanding.

Proverbs 9:10

Wisdom is the principal thing; therefore get wisdom; and with all thy getting get understanding.

Proverbs 4:7

If any of you lack wisdom, let him ask of God, that giveth to all men liberally, and upbraideth not; and it shall be given him.

James 1:5

Bibliography

Barnes, Emilie with Anne Christian Buchanan. *Help me Trust you God,* Eugene, Oregon: Harvest House Publishers, 1998.

Dunn, Ronald. *When Heaven is silent,* Nashville, Tennessee: Thomas Nelson, Inc., 1994.

George, Elizabeth. *A Woman's Call to Prayer,* Eugene, Oregon: Harvest House Publishers, 2004.

Greene, Donna. *Growing godly women – A Christian Women's Guide to Mentoring Teenage Girls,* Birmingham, Alabama: New Hope Publishers, 2002.

Heward-Mills, Dag. *Daughter You Can Make It,* Accra-Ghana, London-UK: Parchment House, 2006.

Heward-Mills, Dag. *Lay People and the Ministry,* Accra-Ghana, London-UK: Parchment House, 1999.

Heward-Mills, Dag. *Name It! Claim It! Take It!* Accra-Ghana, London-UK: Parchment House, 1999.

Heward-Mills, Dag. *The Art of Hearing, following the voice of God,* Accra-Ghana, London-UK: Parchment House, 2001.

Heward-Mills, Dag. *The Art of Leadership,* Accra-Ghana, London-UK: Parchment House, 2003.

Heward-Mills, Dag. *Win the Lost At any Cost,* Accra-Ghana, London-UK: Parchment House, 2001.

Meyer, Joyce. *Beauty for Ashes-Receiving Emotional, Healing* Tulsa, Oklahoma: Harrison House, Inc. 1994.

Meyer, Joyce. *Straight Talk,* New York Boston Nashville: Warner Faith, 2004.

Meyer, Joyce. *The Secret To True Happiness – Enjoy Today, Embrace Tomorrow,* London: Hodder & Stoughton, 2008.

Omartian, Stormie. *Lord I want to be whole*, Nashville, Tennesse: Thomas Nelson, Inc., 2001.

Omartian, Stormie. *Just Enough Light for the Step I'm On*, Eugene, Oregon: Harvest House Publishers, 1999.

Osteen, Joel. *Your best Life Now,* New York Boston Nashville: Warner Faith, 2004.

Osteen, Joel. *Become a Better You,* New York, London, Toronto, Sydney: Free Press, 2007.

Price, Frederick K.C. *How to believe God for A Mate,* Los Angeles, California: Faith One Publishing, 1987.

Wilkinson, Bruce. *The Prayer of Jabez, Breaking through to a blessed life,* Sisters, Oregon: Multnomah Publishers, Inc.

Wright, H.Norman. *Finding the Perfect Partner,* Eugene, Oregon: Harvest House Publishers,1995.

About the Author

Emefa Toppar is originally from Ghana but has been living in The United Kingdom since 1995. Emefa's desire and passion has always been to write for the Lord.

Emefa's childhood ambition and desire in working for the Foreign Service eventually led her to work for almost twelve years in London, with the Commonwealth Secretariat, the main intergovernmental agency and central institution of the Commonwealth of Nations, an intergovernmental organisation of fifty-four independent member states.

She currently works as a Financial Controller, Head of Administration and Chancery with The Order of St John, an International Christian Charity in the United Kingdom.

She has an MBA from the University of Hull, United Kingdom as well as a BA (Hons) and a post graduate diploma in education, from the University of Cape Coast, Ghana.

Her greatest joy now however, is the opportunity she has to serve as a Lay Pastor in the Church.